2012

ECONOMIC DEPRESSION

TIPS ON WEATHERING THE STORM

SANDRA VOYKIN SOUKEROFF

Balboa Press books may be ordered through booksellers or by contacting:

Balboa Press
A Division of Hay House
1663 Liberty Drive
Bloomington, IN 47403
www.balboapress.com
1-(877) 407-4847

Because of the dynamic nature of the Internet, any web addresses or links contained in this book may have changed since publication and may no longer be valid. The views expressed in this work are solely those of the author and do not necessarily reflect the views of the publisher, and the publisher hereby disclaims any responsibility for them.

Any people depicted in stock imagery provided by Thinkstock are models, and such images are being used for illustrative purposes only. Certain stock imagery © Thinkstock.

ISBN: 978-1-4525-3239-4 (sc)

Printed in the United States of America

Balboa Press rev. date: 2/18/2011

Cover design and interior images by Alyse Kirsten Soukeroff

BALBOA.
PRESS
A DIVISION OF HAY HOUSE

If you are presently reading this, you, like myself, are questioning, wondering, and perhaps may even be feeling a bit of anxiety about what really will happen in 2012. Will we witness the Great Depression one worse than the depression of 1929 as some economic gurus have warned of? Or is this all just a media hype, as so many things are these days.

Do you remember the year 2000 scare? Where we were fed information about the Internet being shut down, trucks not being able to bring in food. Our electricity would be cut off due to computer shut downs and on and on. For some of us, this threat to our existence as we knew it, was quite real.

I knew of people that stocked their cupboards with food, bought expensive outdoor electrical generators, and held their breath, so-to-speak, waiting for the witching hour. Well that hour came and went and nothing occurred, other than some annoying Internet computer viruses and life went on. So why would we be questioning the occurrence of a great depression when all other Dooms Day predictions have not transpired?

The economic downturn!

The American housing bubble finally burst. Was this predicted? Absolutely. Did homeowners, investors take heed? Absolutely not.

Who would of ever thought that tent cities would be popping up in California and other states? Homeowners just walking away from their homes because of an inability to pay their mortgages. Many American banks closed, insurance institutions and multi billion dollar corporations that have been around since the 1930's went bankrupt.

Does this not resemble the beginnings of depression? We keep hearing recession, recession, why? Because no one wants to hear the word *depression.* When you hear the word recession, what's your mental picture like? A slow economy, a few lost jobs, just a slow period for the economy and it will soon pick up and the economy will be back to where it was, or maybe even better.

Now, what's your mental picture when you hear the words, Economic Depression? Oh My Goodness! I have so many negative things going on in my head that I think I'm having a panic attack: Banks shutting down with all our money in it! Grocery stores with empty shelves, losing my job, my husband losing his job. How do we pay our mortgage now that interest rates have tripled? How do we put food on the table?

Yes, the word depression really does mean depression. (*Dictionary definition: the act of depressing; or a state of being depressed; low spirits or vitality; a low or depressed place or surface; a severe decline in business, accompanied by increasing unemployment, falling prices, etc.)* What a nasty little word. How can one little word make you feel like the world is crashing in around you? Maybe that is the purpose of talking recession instead of depression. Recession! What a nice little word. Everything is going to be okay. For the rest of this book, I will be referring to the word depression as the "D" word.

Regardless of what word we use, the global economy is in a tailspin and we are in the middle of it. So what are you going to do? Do you just sit back and see where the chips fall and pick up the pieces or do you take action. Actions that can rid some of the anxiety that you are feeling. Do you prepare or not?

When the meteorologist on your local news announces that a storm is coming your way, does he/she not tell you to prepare? When a hurricane is coming your way, do you board up your homes in preparation? Or do you just sit back and watch the hurricane destroy your home and family. Do you pray that the meteorologists are wrong and pray that the storm will change course and spare your home and belongings?

Of course you board up your home!! You get drinking water, canned food prepared, you prepare a medical kit, you have candles and flashlights ready, you ensure all your family and pets are secured in your home. Yes, you PREPARE. Same as the predicted coming of the 'D', are you going to prepare or are you going to pray that it won't happen.

Throughout the next sections, I will provide you with tips on hopefully riding out the storm.

PREPARE

Money, money, money, oh for the sake of the old dollar that keeps our little world turning. I use 'little world' because even though distance wise, the world is vast whether you live in Salt Lake City, Utah, or you live in Istanbul, Turkey, the common thread is money. We are all so very connected through this commodity. This is precisely the reason why we have witnessed a Global Recession; every country is in some way connected to each other through the means of money.

If each country was truly autonomous, we would not be speaking of a Global Recession, it would be individual countries suffering their own downturn. Many individuals had their retirement income investments based on the American housing market, when that crashed so did their investments, even though these investors were residents of other countries. There went their buying power creating a domino effect of lack of consumer spending. It would be a huge mistake to think, "Oh, that won't happen in my country, our economy is stable."

Globally, Nationally, Locally connected, yes we are all connected through money.

EMPLOYMENT

Have you thought of what you would do if one day you went to your office feeling quite secure about your position, only to be called in for a special morning meeting to be told that your job is being cut due to down sizing or closing. How would you react? Shock, anger, anxiety, helplessness, or would you accept it and move on.

For the majority of people, it would probably be one of the first 4 reactions and for a minority, it will be the last reaction, "I'll move on." Why the difference in reactions? The difference being that the 'minority' was prepared. The 'I'll move on' group has an established array of marketable skills. They have the ability to seek jobs in different fields. They are not limited. If for the last 15 years you have worked as a Battery Engineer and that is all the skills that you possess, odds are that you will probably have a difficult time finding a job in that same field. But if you were a Battery Engineer, with some additional skills in the trades, computer, sales, the chances of you finding another job would be much higher.

TIPS:

- Take additional courses.
- Search job banks for fields that are in demand.
- Upgrade existing skills.
- Look for government grants that support re-training.
- Be creative, take a moment to find what your hidden talents are and act on them.

RAINY DAY FUNDS

Should you find yourself in the position of losing your job or having your wages reduced, would you have the 'ability to pay' (a famous banker term) when you apply for a loan. I am speaking of 'ability to pay' in terms of, "Can you sustain your lifestyle with a lower wage?" Do you have money put aside?

In the last 'D', people didn't trust the banks with their money as banks closed their doors and the people were unable to access their funds. Their money locked. Why do we hear of past stories where people dug up their money, stuffed money inside their mattresses (bad idea) or stashed their money in home safes? The answer is fear! Fear of a repeat of not being able to access their hard earned money. Do you think the Forbes list of Fortune 500 millionaires have all their money held in banks? I would venture to say No. Do they have a rainy day stash? I venture to say yes.

GOLD CRAZE

With gold at an all time high, people are cashing in. Numerous companies can be found on the Internet and T.V. wanting to buy your gold jewelry, be it sound pieces, broken or bullion. They **want** it and they will send you cash immediately.

Is it worthwhile to sell your gold now and make money? I guess that would depend on what you actually need the money for. Are you selling your gold to raise money for a tropical vacation? Or are you selling your gold to make your next months mortgage payment. In any event perhaps it would be wise to hold onto your gold for now. It has been predicted that if there is another 'D', you just might be using your gold to buy bread!

My father lived through the Depression and to this day, he is still telling us to pay off the mortgage, don't get into debt, save your money. I guess for once in my life, I am beginning to take his advice.

TIPS

- Every month put money away, some in the bank to gain interest, some, where it is easily accessible.
- Pay down your mortgage.
- Consolidate your loans – free up money.
- Start group savings account (friends/family).
- Roll up spare coins laying around (amazing what it adds up to).
- Limit use of credit cards.
- Budget, budget, budget!
- Don't try to 'keep up with the Jones.'

So the 'D' is here, you have a job, but you only make enough to pay your mortgage and utilities with a small amount left over for food. What do you do? How do you put a meal on the table for your family when you have limited funds?

We are witnessing this situation currently in the Global Recession. The demand for food banks has sharply risen from past years. More and more people are relying on food banks to get them through the months. Yet contributions have declined. If this was to happen to you, would you be reliant on the food banks or would you be self sufficient. If you are not self-sufficient as of today, you can easily start becoming self-sufficient today.

How? PREPARE

I'd like you to get up right now, walk over to your fridge, and open it up. What do you see inside? Do you see Tupperware containers filled with leftovers from the night before, a dozen eggs, a brick of cheese, milk, and jam? Or do you see a few cans of pop, beer, left over take-out boxes from pizza, burger places or other fast food establishments.

If it's the latter, we seriously need to ***chat.***

One of my long time frustrations is that most people really don't know how to shop for food! There have been so many times where I would look at the grocery carts of individuals in the cashier line up and would *cringe* at the sight of their purchases.

Their purchases, in my view, were totally unhealthy and costly. The only thing stopping me from approaching the grocery shopper and commenting on their purchases was having created a *scene* at the grocery store, when the individual would probably say, "Mind your own business lady, it's my food". So I reluctantly turn my head and concentrate on my own grocery cart.

The retailers have done an excellent job of promoting their packaged ready-made food to us the consumer. They have cleverly researched our busy lifestyles and have created numerous products that we can purchase and have ready in 15 or 20 minutes. All for the sake of 'saving time'. Time that we somehow run out of during the day, hence we prepare supper as quickly as we can.

I assume that this is what the consumer is looking for, but what if you are on a budget? What if all the money you had for 1 weeks worth of food would only pay for one supper of pre-made packaged food? We need to change the way we purchase food to reflect times of economic struggle.

For instance, you can purchase 1 package of macaroni and cheese for approximately $1.00, which would be enough for 1 meal. Or you can purchase a 2kg box of macaroni for $6.00 which would last you for 16 meals. I measured the contents of both.

> Macaroni & cheese box   = 1 3/4 cups uncooked
>
> Macaroni – 2kg   = 16 cups uncooked

Even though you pay 6 times the amount for the 2 kg box you are still ahead by 5.5 cups of macaroni. That is 5.5 extra meals.

The same can be said for potatoes, and carrots. Why purchase a small bag of frozen ready made potatoes or carrots when you can purchase a 5lb bag of carrots or potatoes that would give you more meals for your dollar.

If the "D" does transpire, one of two things will likely occur or maybe both: food will be inflated and/or limited.

Preparing now can give you a peace of mind that if and when you need it, it is there. You will have no need to panic, because you already have food.

TIPS

- Every time you go grocery shopping, purchase extra canned foods, preferably something that is on sale like (beans, vegetable, fish, meats, tomatoes).
- Avoid the grocery store isles.
- Purchase a sack of rice (store in freezer, it can last 5-6 years may be even longer).
- Purchase salt, and sugar (seal salt in old wine bottles, put a tsp of rice on top to draw out moisture.)
- Purchase packages of dried beans, barley, lentils, and/or pasta.
- Dehydrate fruits and store.
- Learn to cook with simple ingredients.
- Purchase cookbooks, and cook at home.

STOCK UP, DON'T HOARD

With a variety of home renovation reality programs on television, I always turn to the program with the outdoor projects, yard renovations in particular as I prefer to spend as much time as I can outdoors, and I try to get ideas.

I am always impressed with the yard transformations, how the yard specialists turn a weedy, dirt and rock filled back yard into a beautiful, eye catching work of art, complete with water ponds, pools, cement tiled patios, and flower beds. While for now it serves the purpose, how will these beautiful yards fair when the "D" is here.

I can recall a few years ago, I purchased (as usual) flats of bedding flowers to plant in my yard and create hanging flower baskets. After spending a few days planting and arranging I looked around feeling quite proud of my creations and my yard.

Then my mother and father dropped by for a visit. Being proud of my flower creations I proceeded to show my parents. I said, "Look at my flower gardens, aren't they beautiful?" I asked. My mother turned to me and said, "Yes my dear they are so very beautiful, but can you eat them?" (Meaning, perhaps you should be spending your time planting something that you can eat instead of something to just look at). My next project, yes you guessed it, was planting an edible garden.

While visiting a friend who is a retired psychologist, he told me that during wartime, Britain fed the nation by transforming the city parks into vegetable gardens. What a creative way to feed your people.

So, instead of beautifying your surroundings with just flowers, shrubs, ponds, cement walkways, perhaps a more sustainable project like creating a garden filled with vegetables would be more beneficial.

TIPS

- Learn to garden.
- If you have a yard, designate an area for gardening.
- If you live in an apartment (with a balcony) plant vegetables in pots.
- If you live in a condo/penthouse suite with a terrace, create a mini garden.
- Collaborate with your neighbours; organize a neighbourhood vegetable exchange where each household would grow only one vegetable (preferably a high yield such as tomatoes, cucumbers, green beans, carrots, raspberry, strawberries, etc.) and once a week portion out the vegetables per household.
- Learn to preserve vegetables.
- Plant a variety of mints, dry your own teas.

Gardening actually serves two purposes: One, it provides you with life sustaining food and Two, is quite therapeutic. There is something quite calming and humbling in performing the simple act of sticking your hands in dirt and planting one tiny seed.

Rewarding when you see that first sign of plant life pop its little head through the dirt and transform itself into a beautiful vegetable that you can pick and put on your dinner table.

I'm feeling stressed. I'm depressed. My nerves are shot! I can't deal with this anymore!

Had a bad day at work? Your pay cheque doesn't cover the bills? Can't find a job?

I think I'll have a drink!!

Does this sound familiar? I'm sure it does. All too often when we are in crisis mode, we need a quick fix. We don't know how to resolve the present crisis, so out comes the 'faithful old friend', always there for you, doesn't argue, and above all is unconditional.

But unfortunately has a price, a high price: your **Physical and Emotional Well-Being**.

Substance abuse is prevalent in our society costing millions in treatment, and rehabilitation. Taxing health care and creating an influx of criminal activity resulting in a back log of court cases.

In tough economic times, when jobs are scarce, whom do you think an employer would be more likely to hire? An individual with a substance abuse problem or an individual that exercises sobriety?

Employers seek workers that are committed, have a high degree of work ethics and expect maximum production levels from their employees. These are the types of people that in tough times will still be able to obtain employment.

Employers will not be interested in employees that miss work days because of hangovers, alcohol binges, or individuals that have developed some form of psychosis due to their prolonged use of hallucinogens (marijuana, ecstasy, hashish), stimulants (cocaine, methamphetamine) or prescription drugs.

All too often in today's society individuals presenting with substance abuse problems rely on the so called "system" to help them. The human rights act views addiction as a disability, therefore creating a "duty to accommodate" scenario for the employer and a social service responsibility for the government.

Once it is established that an individual does have an addiction problem, they are recommended for treatment (at the employers/ government cost) in hopes of rehabilitating the individual.

The reality is that until the affected individuals make the decision to help themselves, treatment and rehabilitation will have little or no affect.

The reality is that you have to help yourself and not rely on the 'system' to make changes for you. The 'system' is only there as a safety net, only a temporary net, one designed to, after a short time be pulled out from under your feet. The system cannot change your destructive behavior unless you take control of your own life and make the change.

TIPS

- Coping skills (learn new coping to combat your emotional reactions).
- Find out what your *triggers* are.
- Listen to music; purchase a music therapy book, tapes, etc.
- Start a physical exercise routine.
- Go for a walk around the block (simple first step).
- Find a support group.
- Find a hobby.
- Don't be idle.
- Become a volunteer, volunteer in your community, or a global community.
- Seek out counseling service.

We have now come to the end of this little guide of tips. I could easily write many, many more pages, as I have a lot to say, but my intention was to create something that would be an easy, quick read. One where you can take the suggested tips and start applying them immediately.

Far too often I have purchased books (lengthy ones at that) spent time reading them, become inspired at certain parts of the book but by the conclusion of the book have failed to *act* on these inspirations.

Hopefully through some part, you have found something inspirational, something that you can begin to do today or in the very near future to help reduce your levels of anxiety, put yourself and family at ease that if and when the "D" does in fact rear it's ugly little head, you will be PREPARED and we can collectively ride out the *storm.*

You need only to keep one word in your mind.   **PREPARE**.

I have prepared this guide in the hope that some of my homespun logic and experience may be useful to readers with questioning, wondering minds.